This notebook belongs to:

____

Made in the USA
Columbia, SC
06 August 2024

40067585R00068